The A - Z of
TEEN TALK

Lucy van Amerongen

ЯR
RAVETTE PUBLISHING

First published by Ravette Publishing 2007.

Ravette Publishing Limited
Unit 3, Tristar Centre
Star Road, Partridge Green
West Sussex RH13 8RA

ISBN: 978-1-84161-291-1

INTRODUCTION

Are you like a teenager? Do you like have teenage children? Or do you like work with or meet teenagers?

If so you will need this little dictionary to help you understand what we're saying.

That's because over the last few years we've developed our own language that's so fit.

It's not difficult - but just remember the three BIG RULES:

1) If talking to an adult (like one of your rents) never make eye contact as it suggests you might be vaguely interested in anything they're saying.

2) Always mumble inaudibly. That's 'cos it suggests you've got ATTITUDE.

3) If possible include the word "like" in like every sentence.

So read on, enjoy and soon you too could be fluent in TEEN TALK!!!

Whatever.

About the Author

Lucy van Amerongen is a teenager, innit?

A

ace   smart, cool. Can also be used as a verb, as in "I aced that test".

ag   abbreviation of aggravate. "She really ags me."

ah nam   tell on someone, rat on them.

antwacky   unstylish, unfashionable, old-fashioned.

arvo   abbreviation of afternoon, as in "See you tomorrow arvo".

B

bait   a general negative word, as in "That's so bait".

bare   a lot of, very.

batties   trousers. q.v. **kecks**. Someone who wears their trousers too low down is doing a "batty ride".

beast (1)   an adjective to describe something that's really cool.

beast (2)   a verb that means to do something quickly. "As soon as you hear the bell, beast it over to the tuck shop."

begging   talking rubbish.

bezzie/bez   best friend

big up   to praise.

bitch up   to be denigrated or maligned by a female person. "She used to be heavy, but then she bitched me up big time."

biter   someone who copies something from someone else.

bo   really cool. Not as cool as **fit**, but more cool than **neat**.

book   an adjective to describe something that's really cool. That's because it's the first option given in predictive text when typing 'c o o l'.

boom boom   a term of approval, particularly in London.

brap   cool, wicked.

bruv	mate, friend.
buff	sexy, fit. Particularly when describing boys.
bum	enjoy. Example: "He bums his PS2 wicked."
butt out	go away.
butters	ugly. But not with necessarily abusive meaning, as in the farewell phrase **laters butters** (q.v.).
buzzing	cool.

C

chat talk back, contradict, as in "Don't chat to me!"

checkers clothes.

chirp chat up. "He chirped some **buff** girls las' nite."

chud chewing gum.

chung extremely sexy.

clappin' out of date, worn out. Usually used to describe an object or item of clothing, but can be used to describe a relationship that's passed its sell-by date.

cool original and still most widely used term of approval for anything and everything.

cotch down   hang out, chill or sleep. Thought to derive from the French word for sleep, coucher.

creps   trainers. See also **trabs** and **kicks**.

crew   your mates.

crump   a general term that usually means something's bad, but in the best traditions of Teen Talk it can also mean good!

cruzer   someone with a car.

D

da bomb   great, excellent.

dash   to pass something to someone.

dis   to disrespect, mock or ridicule.

dred   dreadful, terrible.

dry   dull, boring, stupid, unfunny.

E

elm   stupid person. "He got 1% in his mocks - what an elm!"

elton   a toilet. Derived from the fact that "john" means this in America, and the name of a well-known pop star.

ends   area, estate. As in "What ends are you from?"

ernie   stupid person. Alternative to **elm** or **panwit** - but not as stupid as a **fudge**.

F

feds police, Derived from the American FBI.

fetch really attractive. Even more so than **fit**.

fit good-looking, sexy. Ultimately the most over-used expression for approval of a human male.

flash great, not bad.

flat roofin' to be overworked and stressed, as in "I was flat roofin' for my GCSEs".

fo sho for sure. Urban term of affirmation.

fudge a very, very stupid person. One theory is that it derives from the grades achieved at GCSE by some unfortunate loser.

G

gash unpleasant, ugly.

gay annoying, as in "It's so gay, I have too much homework".

gaylord annoying person.

go say. Used in conjunction with **like** to describe a typical teen conversation:
I'm like: "Are you coming to the club?"
And he goes: "Yuh, maybe."
So I'm like: "Well are you?"
And he goes: "No."

gratz thank you.

grimy good. Not as good as **mint** but better that **neat**.

H

hangin'	ugly. "I fink you should **unass** him as he's well hangin."
heavy	cool, interesting.
hench	strong, tough - particularly to describe a boy.
hot	another word for sexy.
howling	extremely ugly.

I

ice   jewellery.

igry   embarrassed. "Stop doing that, you're making me igry."

innit   word which when added to the end of any sentence turns it into a question. "Robbie Williams is right **rinsed**, innit?"

J

jack   to take or steal, as in "car-jacking".

jamming   hanging around.

jokes   funny or enjoyable, as in "that party was jokes".

jook   variant of **jack**. "You only got those **grimy creps** 'cos you jooked them!"

K

kecks   trousers. q.v. **batties**.

kicks   pair of shoes or trainers.

klingon   younger child - particularly your irritating brother or sister.

kotch   hang out, chill or sleep. Alternative spelling to **cotch**.

kronik   something really bad.

L

lairy loud. "Don't get lairy with me!"

laoy dat forget that. Expression used in Birmingham.

laters butters goodbye, see you.

ledge a legend, someone who is greatly admired.

leg it to run away as fast as possible.

like means anything and everything you want. But in particular can be used to mean 'say' (as with **go**).

long can't be bothered, won't make an effort.

lush good-looking, sexy, cool.

M

mackin' out   relaxing, chilling.

majestik   really **wicked**, extremely **nang**.

mank   bad, ugly, horrible. It's amazing how many words we have that basically express the same idea.

ming   bad, ugly, horrible. The most over-used term of negativity, suitable for inclusion in a high percentage of teenage expressions of opinion.

minger   the person who is **ming**. Most people (particularly adults) are mingers in teenage eyes. According to the BBC News website, this expression dates back to 1995.

minging   alternative to **ming**.

ming-mong   actually means the opposite of ming, i.e. cool, attractive.

mint   cool, first rate.

minted   really rich. For example, some celebrities go on luxurious holidays 'cos they are well minted.

morwan   boring. Apparently derived from a regional Chinese language.

mouldies   parents. Abbreviation for mouldy oldies. See also **rents**.

munter   ugly. An alternative to **minger**, which is now a bit uncool.

N

nang   cool, excellent, brilliant.

neat   quite attractive, but not as
             strong as **mint**.

nim nim nim   description for what's said when
             someone is speaking rubbish, as
             in "my rents were telling me off
             . . . nim nim nim!".

nuff   really, very.

O

off the hook   cool, appealing, fresh. Usually
preceded by totally or proper.

oudish   very good, excellent, wicked.

owned   to be made a fool of, to be
beaten by.

P

pantypop   the act of passing wind.

panwit   someone who's stupid, thick, brainless.

phat   really cool, great, awesome.

phat-free   uncool, rubbish, the opposite to **phat**.

pie   to ignore, cut dead.

piggin'   eating, stuffing your face.

praise!   that's great, thank you.

pump down   calm down.

punk   to fool or dupe someone. "Ha, ha – you've been punked!"

R

rago   whatever, OK, allow it.

rank   really bad, filthy, obnoxious.

rare   ugly, unpleasant (describing a person).

rents   parents. As in "Jane's party was **grimy** - till her rents came back early".

rinsed (1)   worn out, finished, something that's had its day.

rinsed (2)   proved wrong.

roll with   hang out with.

S

safa   very cool, superlative version of **safe**.

safe   cool, good, sweet.

scav   borrow or steal. Derived from scavenger. "Can I scav a toffee?"

sexy   attractive, desirable, but usually when referring to an object rather than a person.

shabby   cool, smart. A word that now means the opposite of how our **rents** would use it.

shizzle   someone who you worship, as in "she's a real shiz".

sick	interesting, cool. Another word that now has the opposite meaning.
skank	variant of **mank.**
slap up	beat up, attack.
slate	abbreviation of "See you later".
soz	sorry. The variant sozzard is used in Devon.
splinked	drunk. "He's well splinked up."
stoked	happy.
sup?	abbreviation of "What's up?"
swag	extreme, scary, frightening.
switch	to turn against someone.

T

tear to leave quickly, run away. "You ready to go? Then let's tear."

the bomb cool, awesome, the best. Variant of **da bomb**.

tight description of close relationship, as in "We're close friends, we're tight".

tin-grin rude name for someone who wears braces.

trabs trainers.

trump to pass wind. "Who trumped?"

U

uber   very, totally. A German word we
                 use to show our mastery of
                 foreign languages.

unass   to relinquish or surrender
                 control of an object or person.

V

vanilla boring, dull – particularly when referring to someone's taste in clothes. "Look at her **checkers** – vanilla or what?"

vexed irritated, angry. An old English word that has come back into Teen Talk.

vurp a belching action that's somewhere between vomiting and burping.

vut idiot, loser, time-waster. "Don't go out with him - he's such a vut."

W

wafwaan
what's up? What's going on?
Originally from Jamaican slang.

wag
abscond, skive. "He wagged off
school yesterday."

wallace
vomit. A new piece of rhyming
slang based on Wallace and
Gromit. q.v. **yarf**.

wazz
to apply make-up. If someone is
having a makeover or beauty
treatment she is being wazzed
up.

well
very. "She is well **ming**!"

wet
very good, excellent, cool.

whatever
a one-word answer to anything
we don't want to talk about.

wicked extremely desirable. Much more desirable than **lush**, **nang**, **mint** or **shabby**.

word hole mouth.

wuss coward, wimp, loser.

Y

yard   house, garden, the place where you live or hang out.

yarf   vomit. A new variant on the word barf.

yoot   child, children.

Z

za
abbreviation of pizza.
"Let's grab a za before the movie."

zep
oik, yob, person from the underclass.

zoinks!
exclamation of surprise. Originally used in the Scooby-Doo cartoon series.

ACKNOWLEDGEMENTS

I am like indebted to the following for providing suggestions and additional material:

Amii van Amerongen and Rosie van Amerongen (my sisters)

Chloe Hawkey

BBC News E-cyclopedia

BBC Radio Devon

The Nordic Journal of Youth Research, Swedish Science Press, Uppsala

The Online Dictionary of Playground Slang (ODPS)

Pragmatic Markers in Teenage and Adult Conversation; G. Andersen, University of Bergen, Norway

If you've got like a word to add to my A-Z,
then get in touch with me.

My email address is ...

lucyvanam@hotmail.com

Lucy